The Story of a Special Day
Volume 67

March 7

66th day of the year
(67th in leap years)
299 days remaining
until the end of the year.

by Michael Dobson

Timespinner
Press

For more information about the series, about me, or about your special day, please email us at editor@timespinnerpress.com.

Look for other volumes in *The Story of a Special Day,* coming often.

Table of Contents

Cover: "Gray Tree" by Piet Mondrian, born March 7, 1872.

Back Cover: The Ludendorff Bridge at Remagen, captured by US troops during World War II on March 7-8, 1945

March 7 Quotations

"Let us come out into the light of day; let us enjoy the fresh airs of Liberty and Union; let us cherish those hopes which belong to us; let us devote ourselves to those great objects that are fit for our consideration and our action; let us raise our conceptions to the magnitude and the importance of the duties that devolve upon us; let our comprehension he as broad us the country for which we act, our aspirations as high as its certain destiny; let us not be pygmies in a case that calls for men."

— Daniel Webster, "Seventh of March" speech, given on March 7, 1850

"The surface of things gives enjoyment, their interiority gives life."

— Piet Mondrian, artist, born March 7, 1872

"When I was bullied: you manned-up. You learned something. You realized: I'm not getting the gold star. You realized: you lose. Deal with it."

— *Bret Easton Ellis, author, born March 7, 1964*

"Three things are necessary for the salvation of man: to know what he ought to believe; to know what he ought to desire; and to know what he ought to do."

— *Saint Thomas Aquinas, died March 7, 1274*

"The most terrifying fact about the universe is not that it is hostile but that it is indifferent; but if we can come to terms with this indifference and accept the challenges of life within the boundaries of death — however mutable man may be able to make them — our existence as a species can have genuine meaning and fulfillment. However vast the darkness, we must supply our own light."

— *Stanley Kubrick, director, died March 7, 1999*

The Bridge at Remagen

As Allied forces approached the Rhine River, the last natural barrier protecting the German heartland, soldiers of the Third Reich worked feverishly to destroy all the bridges the Allies could use to cross the river. By early March, only two bridges remained, one near the town of Remagen, the other near Wesel.

On March 7, 1945, elements of the U.S. Army's 9th Armored Division reached the Ludendorff Bridge at Remagen, and were surprised to discover that the bridge, although damaged, was not yet destroyed. A token force of some 36 German soldiers were busily wiring explosives. They had received only 300 kg of explosives rather than the 600 kg they had requested.

At 1340 hours, the Americans attacked, and the German defenders set off the first charge, tearing a crater in the left bank ramp, and two hours later they set off the main

4

explosion. The entire bridge lifted up slightly, then dropped back into place because a failure of one wire leading to the explosives.

Quickly, the leading edge of the Allied forces advanced over the bridge: Sgt. Alexander Drabik of Holland, Ohio, became the first American soldier to cross the Rhine into Nazi Germany.

Although the bridge was damaged, it was usable, and within 24 hours, over 8,000 Allied troops crossed into Germany, passing by a sign that read, "Cross the Rhine with Dry Feet, Courtesy of 9th Armd Division."

General Dwight Eisenhower said that the bridge was "worth its weight in gold." The Germans evidently felt the same way, executing four responsible officers by firing squad. Hitler fired Gerd von Rundstedt, the field marshall in charge of the western front.

After the capture, the Germans continued to attack the bridge, sending bombers, artillery, and V-2 rockets. The attacks took their toll; on March 17 the bridge collapsed into the Rhine, killing 18 and injuring 93. However, by then the Allies had established a bridgehead on the far side of the Rhine and had additional pontoon bridges in place.

The 1969 movie *The Bridge at Remagen,* covers the capture of the Ludendorff Bridge. Today, the two surviving towers of the bridge house a museum devoted to peace.

The Ludendorff Bridge after its collapse on March 17, 1945

March 7 Holidays and Celebrations

Teacher's Day (Albania)
Teacher's Day in Albania commemorates the opening of the first secular school teaching lessons in Albanian.

Festival of Vejovis (Ancient Rome)
The ancient Roman god Vejovis was a god of healing. Three festivals were held each year in his honor, January 1, March 7, and May 21, each involving the sacrifice of a female goat.

A Roman silver denarius of 84 BCE showing Vejovis (left)

Christian Feast Days
Saints commemorated on March 7 include Thomas Aquinas, Perpetua and Felicitas.

What Happened on March 7?

321 CE – Sunday Becomes a Day of Rest

Before the establishment of Christianity as the official religion of the Roman Empire, worship of the sun god Sol Invictus ("Invincible Sun") was widespread. Sol Invictus's special day was December 25, and one of the days of the week ("Sun-day") was named for him. Although Jews and early Christians celebrated Saturday as the holy day of rest, the Roman Christian emperor Constantine the Great, decreed that Sunday should be the day of rest in the Empire. Some scholars think that the celebration of Christmas on December 25 is related to Sol Invictus.

1799 CE – Siege of Jaffa Ends

From March 3 to March 7, 1799, the French forces under Napoleon Bonaparte attacked the ancient walled city of Jaffa, in modern Israel. After the fall of the defending towers, Jaffa fell, and Napoleon allowed his soldiers to rape and pillage the town, killing at least 2,400 prisoners.

Napoleon in Jaffa, painted by Antoine-Jean Gross, 1804

1826 CE – **The Shrigley Abduction**

On March 7, 1827, English politician and diplomat Edward Gibbon Wakefield kidnapped 15-year old heiress Ellen Turner, daughter of the High Sheriff of Cheshire, told her that her father had become a fugitive, and explained that if she would marry him, her father would be saved. None of this, of course, was true. He took the girl to Scotland, where marriage laws were less strict, then to Calais, in France, where they were discovered and the girl retrieved. Wakefield was imprisoned for three years and the marriage was annulled by a special Act of Parliament.

1850 CE – Daniel Webster's "Seventh of March" Speech

The Compromise of 1850 was an attempt to head off the looming civil war over the institution of slavery. It contained provisions disliked by both sides, but succeeded in staving off war for more than a decade. One of the key speeches that led to the acceptance of the Compromise was by Massachusetts Senator Daniel Webster. The speech led to his resignation from the senate and the end of his presidential ambitions.

1876 CE – Alexander Graham Bell Patents the Telephone

On March 7, 1875, the U.S. Patent Office issued Patent 174,465 to Alexander Graham Bell for "the method of, and apparatus for, transmitting vocal or other sounds telegraphically...by causing electrical undulations, similar in form to the vibrations of the air accompanying the said vocal or other sound."

1936 CE – Germany Reenters the Rhineland

Under the terms of the 1919 Treaty of Versailles, which ended World War I, Germany was forbidden to "maintain or construct any fortification" along the Rhine. On March 7,

1936, in violation of the treaty, Adolf Hitler ordered 19 German infantry battalions to reoccupy the territory. Although war appeared imminent for a few days, soon the tension dissipated, leaving Nazi Germany in control.

1965 CE – "Bloody Sunday" in Selma, Alabama

In July 1964, Alabama Judge James Hare forbade any gathering of three or more people on any issue involving civil rights or voter registration — it was even forbidden to talk to more than two people at a time on these subjects. Dr. Martin Luther King, Jr., defied the injunction in January 1965, and during a February march to the courthouse, an Alabama state trooper shot and killed a protestor. In response, civil rights activists planned a march from Selma to Montgomery to ask Governor George Wallace about his involvement with the shooting; Wallace denounced the march as a threat to public safety. On March 7, 1965, about 600 civil rights marchers headed east out of Selma, to be confronted by Sheriff Jim Clark and his deputies. Marchers were beaten with nightsticks and gassed. Seventeen marchers were hospitalized, and photographs from the incident appeared in newspapers around the world. A second march on March 9 led to the beatings of three white ministers, one of whom died. The third march, beginning on the 21st, succeeded, reaching Montgomery on the 25th. The Selma marches resulted in a long-term shift in public opinion, and triggered the passage of the Voting Rights Amendment.

Alabama police attack civil rights marchers on "Bloody Sunday"

1985 CE – "We Are the World" Released

In 1985, the supergroup "USA for Africa," written by Michael Jackson and Lionel Richie and produced by Quincy Jones, released its single "We Are the World" with profits to charity. Over 20 million copies were sold worldwide, and the recording won three Grammy Awards.

2009 CE – **Kepler Space Telescope Launched**

On March 7, 2009, the Kepler Space Observatory was launched by NASA from Cape Canaveral. It was designed to discover Earth-sized planets around other stars, and as of December 2011 had discovered over 2,300 extrasolar planets.

Who Was Born
on March 7?

The abbreviation "O.S." on some dates refers to the fact that the Russian Empire did not switch from the Julian to the Gregorian calendar at the same time as the rest of Europe, and therefore some figures have two dates for their birth or death.

People whose original names are not in the Western alphabet have their native names in the appropriate script shown in parenthesis.

Acting and Film

Laura Prepon (March 7, 1980 —)

Actress Laura Prepon is best known for her role as Donna on the Fox sitcom *That '70s Show*.

T. J. Thyne (March 7, 1975 —)

Actor T. J. Thyne is best known for playing Dr. Jack Hodgins on the TV series *Bones*.

Jenna Fischer (March 7, 1974 —)

Actress Jenna Fischer received an Emmy nomination for portraying Pam on the long-running NBC sitcom *The Office*.

Matthew Vaughn (March 7, 1971 —)

Producer and director Matthew Vaughn has directed numerous films, including 2011's *X-Men: First Class.*

Peter Sarsgaard (March 7, 1971 —)

Peter Sarsgaard won the National Society of Film Critics Best Supporting Actor Award for his role in the 2003 film *Shattered Glass.*

Rachel Weisz (March 7, 1970 —)

Academy Award-nominated actress Rachel Weisz is known for her movie and theater roles, but is best known for her leading roles in the films *The Mummy* and *The Mummy Returns.*

Wanda Sykes (March 7, 1964 —)

Writer, comedienne, and actress Wanda Sykes won an Emmy in 1999. She was named by *Entertainment Weekly* as one of the 25 funniest people in America in 2004. She has appeared in numerous films and TV series, and had her own talk show, *The Wanda Sykes Show,* on Fox.

Bill Brochtrup (March 7, 1963 —)

Television and stage actor Bill Brochtrup is best known for his role as the gay administrative aide on the series *NYPD Blue.*

Mary Beth Evans (March 7, 1961 —)

Soap opera star Mary Beth Evans played Kayla Brady on *Days of Our Lives* starting in 1986.

Nick Searcy (March 7, 1959 —)

Television actor Nick Searcy played Deke Slayton in Tom Hanks' miniseries *From the Earth to the Moon.*

Donna Murphy (March 7, 1959 —)

Actress Donna Murphy won two Tony Awards, and played Captain Picard's love interest in 1998's *Star Trek: Insurrection.*

Bryan Cranston (March 7, 1956 —)

Actor Bryan Cranston is best known for his leading role as Walter White in the AMC television series *Breaking Bad.*

John Heard (March 7, 1945 —)

Actor John Heard played the father of Macauley Culkin in the first two *Home Alone* movies.

Daniel J. Travanti (March 7, 1940 —)

Daniel J. Travanti is best known for playing Captain Frank Furillo in the 1980s television series *Hill Street Blues.*

James Broderick (March 7, 1927 — November 1, 1982)

Actor James Broderick was nominated for an Emmy for his role in the television series *Family*, and played an FBI agent in the 1975 film *Dog Day Afternoon.*

Anna Magnani (March 7, 1908 — September 26, 1973)

Italian actress Anna Magnani won the Academy Award for Best Actress for her role in 1955's *The Rose Tattoo. Life* magazine called her "one of the most impressive actresses since Garbo."

Virginia Pearson (March 7, 1886 — June 6, 1958)

Actress Virginia Pearson made 51 films, primarily in the silent era, including a role in the 1925 silent film version of *The Wizard of Oz.*

Madame Sul-Te-Wan (March 7, 1873 — February 1, 1959)

The daughter of freed slaves, Madame Sul-Te-Wan (born Nellie Crawford) became a character actress in the early days of film. She appeared in such films as 1915's *Birth of a Nation* and 1916's *Intolerance.* In spite of the limits of roles for African-American actors, she continued to work well into the talkies era, appearing in a small role in 1933's *King Kong* and a larger role in 1954's *Carmen Jones.* She was posthumously inducted into the Black Filmmakers Hall of Fame in 1986.

Art

Milton Avery (March 7, 1885 — January 3, 1965)

American modern painter Milton Avery's works are part of numerous museum collections.

Milton Avery, "Girl Writing," 1941

Piet Mondrian (March 7, 1872 — February 1, 1944)

Dutch painter Piet Mondrian pioneered a non-representational style of painting known as neo-plasticism, consisting of a white canvas painted with vertical and horizontal black lines and the three primary colors.

Piet Mondrian, "Composition II in Red, Blue, and Yellow," 1930

Business

Michael Eisner (March 7, 1942 —)

Michael Eisner was CEO of the Disney Corporation from 1984 to 2005.

Exploration

Sir Ranulph Fiennes (March 7, 1944 —)

Explorer and adventurer Sir Ranulph Fiennes was named by the *Guinness Book of World Records* as the world's greatest living explorer. He was the first person to visit both the North and South Poles on the surface, and the first to cross Antarctica on foot.

Military

René Gagnon (March 7, 1925 — October 12, 1979)

Marine Corporal René Gagnon was one of the men who appeared in the famous World War II photograph "Raising the Flag on Iwo Jima."

Outline of the figures in the photograph "Raising the Flag on Iwo Jima. René Gascon is second from the right.

Dollard Ménard (March 7, 1913 — January 14, 1997)

Canadian Lieutenant Colonel (later General) Dollard Ménard was wounded five times during the Dieppe Raid, for which he received the Distinguished Service Order (DSO). His exploits inspired a famous Canadian World War II poster.

Canadian World War II poster "Ce qu'il faut pour vaincre"
("What It Takes to Win") featuring Dollard Ménard

22

Reinhard Heydrich (March 7, 1904 — June 4, 1942)

Nazi SS officer Reinhard Heydrich was in charge of the Gestapo and served as one of the chief architects of the Holocaust. Adolf Hitler called him "the man with the iron heart." He was assassinated by a British-trained team of Czech and Slovak soldiers in 1942.

Music

Denyce Graves (March 7, 1964 —)

Opera mezzo-soprano Denyce Graves made her debut at the Metropolitan Opera in 1995. She sang during the 55th Presidential Inauguration and at the National Cathedral service for the victims of 9/11.

Taylor Dayne (March 7, 1962 —)

Pop singer-songwriter Taylor Dayne has had 18 individual songs reach the *Billboard* Top 10 including the #1 hit "Love Will Lead You Back."

Ernie Isley (March 7, 1952 —)

Member of The Isley Brothers, prolific songwriter and multi-instrumentalist Ernie Isley wrote such hits as "Brown Eyed Girl" and others.

The Isley Brothers were inducted into the Rock and Roll Hall of Fame in 1992.

Peter Wolf (March 7, 1946 —)

Peter Wolf was the lead vocalist for the J. Geils Band from 1967 to 1983.

Townes Van Zandt (March 7, 1944 — January 1, 1997)

Texas country-folk singer and songwriter Townes Van Zandt died from health problems related to years of substance abuse. His music has been covered by Bob Dylan, Lyle Lovett, and other notable musicians.

Maurice Ravel (March 7, 1875 — December 28, 1937)

French composer Maurice Ravel is best known for his 1928 orchestral work *Boléro*.

Politics

Champ Clark (March 7, 1850 — March 2, 1921)

Missouri congressman Champ Clark was Speaker of the U. S. House of Representatives from 1911 to 1919, and an unsuccessful candidate for the Democratic presidential nomination in 1912.

Publius Septimus Geta (March 7, 189 — Decemer 19, 211)

Publius Septium Geta was the 23rd emperor of the Roman Empire. He co-ruled with his father Septimus Severus and his older brother Caracalla.

Public Figures

Tammy Faye Bakker (March 7, 1942 — July 20, 2007)

Televangelist Tammy Faye Bakker was best known for co-hosting *The PTL Club* with her husband, later convicted felon, Jim Bakker.

Willard Scott (March 7, 1934 —)

Media personality Willard Scott is best known as the weatherman on *The Today Show* and for creating the character of Ronald McDonald for the eponymous hamburger chain.

Lord Snowdon (March 7, 1930 —)

Photographer Antony Armstrong-Jones, 1st Earl of Snowdon, is best known for his first marriage to Princess Margaret, sister of Queen Elizabeth II.

Rob Roy (March 7, 1671 [baptism] — December 28, 1734)

Robert Roy MacGregor, commonly known as Rob Roy, was a Scottish folk hero and outlaw, sometimes referred to as the "Scottish Robin Hood." Originally a cattleman, Rob Roy lost his fortune when his chief herder disappeared, and was branded an outlaw by the Duke of Montrose. Rob Roy fought a private war against the duke until he was forced to surrender in 1722. A fictionalized account of his life, *The Highland Rogue,* turned him into a legend in his own time, and King George I pardoned him for his crimes.

Science

Alan Hale (March 7, 1958 —)

American astronomer Alan Hale is known for co-discovering Comet Hale-Bopp, the most widely observed comet of the 20th century.

Comet Hale-Bopp, by E. Kolmhofer and H. Rabb, Johannes
Kepler Observatory, Linz, Austria

Daniel Goleman (March 7, 1946 —)

Psychologist and science journalist Daniel
Goleman is known for his best-selling 1995 book
Emotional Intelligence.

Olga Aleksandrovna Ladyzhenskaya (Óльга Алексáндровна Ладыженская) (March 7, 1922 — January 12, 2004)

Soviet mathematician Olga Ladyzhenskaya was awarded the Lomonosov Gold Medal in 2002 for her work on partial differential equations and fluid dynamics.

Luther Burbank (March 7, 1849 — April 11, 1926)

Botanist Luther Burbank, known as the "Wizard of Horticulture," developed more than 800

strains and varieties of plants, including the Elberta Peach, the Santa Rosa Plum, and the Russet Burbank Potato.

Luther Burbank with his spineless cactus, developed for cattle feed.

John Herschel (March 7, 1792 — May 11, 1871)

Son of the astronomer Sir William Herschel, John Herschel made numerous contributions to photography and the investigation of color blindness, and named seven moons of Saturn and four of Uranus.

Nicéphore Niépce (March 7, 1765 — July 5, 1833)

French inventor Nicéphore Niépce developed the world's first internal combustion engine in 1806 and took the first photograph in 1826.

"La cour du domaine du Gras" ("View from the Window at Le Gras"), taken by Nicéphore Niépce, is the first permanent photograph ever taken.

Sports

Jeff Kent (March 7, 1968 —)

Winner of the 2001 National League MVP award and the all-time leader in home runs among second basement, Jeff Kent is a five-time baseball All-Star.

Jesper Parnevik (March 7, 1965 —)

Swedish professional golfer Jesper Parnevik spent 38 weeks in the top 10 of the Official World Golf Ranking in 2000 and 2001.

Steve Beuerlein (March 7, 1965 —)

Former NFL quarterback and CBS analyst Steve Beuerlein led the NFL in passing yards in 1999.

Jim Spivey (March 7, 1960 —)

Middle-distance runner Jim Spivey won a bronze at the 1987 Rome Olympics and a silver at the 1987 Pan American Games.

Ivan Lendl (March 7, 1960 —)

Fomer World No. 1 professional tennis player Ivan Lendl won eight Grand Slam singles titles and 22 Championship Series titles.

Joe Carter (March 7, 1960 —)

Right fielder Joe Carter is best known for hitting a walk-off home run to win the 1993 World Series for the Toronto Blue Jays. It was only the second time a World Series has ended with a home run, and the only time the home run was hit by a player whose team was behind.

Tom Lehman (March 7, 1959 —)

Tom Lehman is the only golfer to win Player of the Year on all three PGA tours.

Tommy Kramer (March 7, 1955 —)

NFL quarterback Tommy Kramer is a member of the College Football Hall of Fame.

Lynn Swann (March 7, 1952 —)

Former Pittsburgh Steeler Lynn Swann was a member of four Super Bowl teams and ran unsuccessfully as the Republican nominee for Governor of Pennsylvania in 2006.

Franco Harris (March 7, 1950 —)

Former Steeler and Seahawk Franco Harris was inducted into the Pro Football Hall of Fame in 1990.

Janet Guthrie (March 7, 1938 —)

Racer Janet Guthrie was the first woman to qualify and compete in the Indianapolis and Dayton 500s.

Janet Guthrie's Wildcat 3-DGS

Ivar Ballangrud (March 7, 1904 — June 1, 1962)

Norwegian Ivar Ballangrud was a four-time Olympic speed skating champion. He won three gold medals in the 1936 Winter Olympics.

Words

Bret Easton Ellis (March 7, 1964 —)

A member of the "literary Brat Pack," author Bret Easton Ellis is best known for his novels *Less Than Zero* and *American Psycho*.

Elizabeth Moon (March 7, 1945 —)

Science fiction writer Elizabeth Moon won the 2003 Nebula Award for her novel *The Speed of Dark*.

Stanley Schmidt (March 7, 1944 —)

Science fiction author and editor Stanley Schmidt is best known for his role as editor of *Analog Science Fiction and Fact* magazine. He has been nominated for the Hugo Award over 30 times, but has never won.

Who Died on March 7?

Acting and Film

Paul Winfield (May 22, 1939 — March 7, 2004)

Oscar and Emmy nominee Paul Winfield is known for his portrayal of a Louisiana sharecropper in *Sounder*, for his portrayal of Dr. Martin Luther King, Jr., in the miniseries *King,* and as a starship commander in *Star Trek: The Wrath of Khan.*

Charles Gray (August 29, 1928 — March 7, 2000)

British actor Charles Gray played Blofield in the James Bond movie *Diamonds are Forever* and the Criminologist in *The Rocky Horror Picture Show.*

Stanley Kubrick (July 26, 1928 — March 7, 1999)

Often listed among the greatest filmmakers of all time, Stanley Kubrick directed such films as *Spartacus, Dr. Strangelove, 2001: A Space Odyssey, A Clockwork Orange,* and *Full Metal Jacket.*

Logo for *2001: A Space Odyssey*

Divine (October 19, 1945 — March 7, 1988)

Cult actor and drag queen Divine starred in ten films by John Waters, most famously 1972's *Pink Flamingos* and 1998's *Hairspray.*

Ben Blue (September 12, 1901 — March 7, 1975)

Comedian and musician Ben Blue appeared in early sound musicals, and had his own TV series in 1950, *The Ben Blue Show.* He appeared regularly on *The Frank Sinatra Show* and owned a popular eponymous nightclub.

Business and Philanthropy

Emanuel Bronner (February 1, 1908 — March 7, 1977)

Dr. Emanuel Bronner developed "Dr. Bronner's Castile Soap," which generated a huge amount of lather from a few drops. He was also noted for his philosophy, the "Moral ABC," and his firm continues to support numerous charitable causes.

Espionage

Sidney Gottlieb (August 3, 1918 — March 7, 1999)

CIA chemist Sidney Gottlieb is known for his work with the MK-ULTRA program that administered LSD and other psychoactive drugs to unwitting subjects for the purpose of mind control and interrogation.

Music

Frankie Carle (March 25, 1903 — March 7, 2001)

Nicknamed "The Wizard of the Keyboard," Frankie Carle's "Sunrise Serenade" was a number one hit in 1938.

Pee Wee King (February 18, 1914 — March 7, 2000)

Country music recording artist and songwriter Pee Wee King is best known as the co-writer of "The Tennessee Waltz" and other hits including "Seven Come Eleven."

Record label from "Seven Come Eleven" by Pee Wee King.

Photography

Gordon Parks (November 30, 1912 — March 7, 2006)

African-American photographer Gordon Parks is best known for his photographic essays in *Life* magazine, and for directing the 1971 film *Shaft*.

Duke Ellington photographed by Gordon Parks

Politics

Jacob Javits (May 18, 1904 — March 7, 1986

Republican Jacob Javits served as United States Senator from New York from 1957 to 1981. New York City's Jacob K. Javits Convention Center is named for him.

Lucy Parsons (c. 1853 — March 7, 1942)

Lucy Parsons, born into slavery of a mixed-race heritage, fled Texas because of persecution for her interracial marriage to a former Confederate soldier. She and her husband, both anarchists, wer active in the early labor movement. After her husband was executed by the state of Illinois in what many regarded as politically trumped-up charges, she joined the Communist Party in 1939 and was known as a powerful orator for radical causes.

Aristide Briand (March 28, 1862 — March 7, 1932)

Eleven-time prime minister of France's Third Republic, Aristide Briand co-won the 1926 Nobel Peace Prize.

Sieur de Bienville (February 23, 1680 — March 7, 1767)

Jean-Baptiste Le Moyne de Bienville was four-time governor of French Louisiana. He is known as a founder of New Orleans, Louisiana; Biloxi, Mississippi; and Mobile, Alabama.

Antonius Pius, Emperor of Rome

Antoninus Pius (September 19, 86 — March 7, 161)

15th emperor of Rome, Antonius Pius had the longest reign since Augustus, serving from 138 to 161.

Public Figures

Mary Josephine Ray (May 17, 1895 — March 7, 2010)

Supercentenarian Mary Josephine Ray was the second-oldest verified living person at the time of her death, and one of the 35 oldest verified people in history. She died shortly before her 115th birthday.

Religion

Paramahansa Yogananda (January 5, 1893 — March 7, 1952)

Yogi and guru Paramahansa Yogananda helped introduce the practices of meditation and yoga to Western audiences through his 1946 book *Autobiography of a Yogi.*

Saint Thomas Aquinas by Filippino Lippi

Saint Thomas Aquinas (c. 1225 — March 7, 1274)

Thomas Aquinas is considered one of the most important theologians and philosophers in

Catholic history, one of only 35 people to be described as "Doctors of the Church." His best-known works include the *Summa Theologiae* and the *Summa Contra Gentiles*. He was proclaimed a saint by Pope John XXII in 1323.

Science

Edward Mills Purcell (August 30, 1912 — March 7, 1997)

Physicist Edward Mills Purcell shared the 1952 Nobel Prize for Physics for his discovery of nuclear magnetic resonance, fundamental to the development of magnetic resonance imaging (MRI).

Robert Abbe (April 13, 1851 — March 7, 1928)

Pioneering surgeon Robert Abbe introduced the practice of using radiation to treat cancer and founded the science of radiation oncology. He also founded the Abbe Museum of Native American Artifacts.

Sports

Cool Papa Bell

Cool Papa Bell (May 17, 1903 — March 7, 1991)

Negro League center fielder Cool Papa Bell is considered to be one of the fastest men ever to play baseball. He was elected to the Baseball Hall of Fame in 1974.

Bradbury Robinson (February 1, 1884 — March 7, 1949)

As a college football player, Bradbury Robinson threw the first legal forward pass in the history of the game. He graduated with a medical degree and served on the staff of the U.S. Surgeon General, where he was one of the first people to argue against the use of DDT in agriculture.

Words

Alice B. Toklas (April 30, 1877 — March 7, 1967)

Alice B. Toklas is famous as the long-time companion of Gertrude Stein. Stein named her own biography *The Autobiography of Alice B. Toklas*. Toklas is also known for her 1954 *The Alice B. Toklas Cookbook,* famous for her recipe for "Haschich Brownies," containing liberal amounts of marijuana.

Wyndham Lewis (November 18, 1882 — March 7, 1977)

Artist and wrter Wyndham Lewis was best known for his leading role in the Vorticist art movement, an offshoot of cubism. He wrote several novels and two autobiographies.

The month of March, from the illuminated manuscript *Les Très Riches Heures du duc de Berry*

March: The Third Month

In ancient Rome, March was the first month of the year. As the first month of spring, in the Mediterranean climate it marked the beginning of the military campaign season. That's why March (Martius) is named in honor of Mars, the Roman god of war.

Although the first month of the year was moved back to January sometime during the transition of Rome from a kingdom to a republic (historians differ), March was the first month of the year in Russia until the end of the 15th Century, and is the first month of the year in many other cultures and religions.

In the northern hemisphere, March 1 marks the beginning of meteorological spring. In the southern hemisphere, March is the equivalent of September, making southern hemisphere March the beginning of autumn.

March is one of the seven months that have 31 days in it. March starts on the same day of the week as November every year, and except for leap years starts on the same day as February. March starts on the same day of the week as the previous June except for leap years, and in leap years starts on the same day as the previous September and December.

March in Other Cultures

In Finland, March is called *maaliskuu* (earthy month). In Ukraine, it's *березень* (birch tree). Other names for March include *Lentmona*t (Saxon), *Hyld-monath* (Angles), and *sušec* (Slovene).

March Symbols

Birthstones: Aquamarine and bloodstone, both representing courage.

Aquamarine

Birth Flowers Daffodils

Daffodils in Bagatelle Park, Paris, France

March Events

Honorary months: Presidents, Congresses, and nations around the world issue proclamations recognizing particular months to honor certain causes. These events generally fall in March. (All US unless otherwise noted.)

- National Nutrition Month
- American Red Cross Month
- Women's History Month (celebrated in Canada during October)
- Irish-American Heritage Month
- Colorectal Cancer Awareness Month
- Fire Prevention Month (The Philippines)

Women's Suffrage picket line, 1917

"March Madness": (United States) The NCAA Men's Division I Basketball Championship, popularly known as "March Madness" or the "Big Dance," is a single-elimination tournament to establish the champion college basketball team.

Multi-day events: Some March events span multiple days.

- **Nineteen Day Fast:** (Bahá'í Faith) March 2 through March 20

Movable events: Some events change dates from year to year.

- **Mardi Gras:** French for "Fat Tuesday," this celebration takes place the day before Ash Wednesday, the beginning of the Lenten season. The New Orleans Mardi Gras celebration is perhaps the most famous, but Mardi Gras and the Carnival season (between Ephiphany and Ash Wednesday) are celebrated in many areas with large Catholic populations. Mardi Gras can take place anywhere from February 3 to March 9 in regular years, and from February 4 to March 9 in leap years.

Mardi Gras Night Parade, New Orleans, 2012

- **Casimir Pulaski Day:** (Illinois) The first Monday in March is observed as a holiday in Illinois, in memory of the Revolutionary War cavalry officer born in Poland. Dates range from March 1 to March 7.

March Zodiac Signs

From the perspective of someone on Earth, the Sun appears to move through the sky throughout the year, along a path astronomers call the ecliptic plane. The ecliptic plane is divided into twelve constellations, known as the zodiac, based on traditionally observed patterns of stars. On your birthday, you can't see your constellation, because it's part of the daytime sky.

The zodiac was first developed by Babylonian astronomers about 2,500 years ago. Because they were unaware that the Earth wobbles like a spinning top (a motion known as *precession*), they didn't make allowance for the fact that the Sun's path through the zodiac changes over time.

That means there are now two sets of dates for your birth sign. The *tropical dates* are the original Babylonian dates; the *siderial dates* tell you where the Sun actually appears as it moves along its annual path.

Zodiac signs for March 7 are Aquarius and Pisces.

Aquarius

Tropical January 20 to February 19
Siderial February 12 to March 8 (March 9 in leap years)

Aquarius is one of the oldest recognized constellations, originally representing the Babylonian god Ea. In Latin, Aquarius means "water-carrier," represented in its symbol. In Greek mythology, Aquarius is sometimes associated with Deucalion, who survived a world-cleansing flood. In Chinese astronomy, it is known as the Black Tortoise of the North (北方玄武, Běi Fāng Xuán Wǔ).

In astrology, Aquarius is considered to be masculine and extroverted, and despite the name is an air sign. Aquarians are supposed to be philanthropical, inventive, and individualistic.

Pisces

Tropical February 20 to March 20
Siderial March 15 to April 14

In the Roman legend of Venus and her son Cupid, they escaped the clutches of Typhon, known as the "father of all monsters," by transforming into fish and tying themselves together with rope. That's why the name Pisces is plural for fish. The constellation appears as a somewhat ragged "V" shape, representing the rope, with the "fish" located at the two rope ends.

In astrology, Pisces is a water sign, compatible with the other water signs Cancer and Scorpio, as well as with the earth signs Taurus, Virgo, and Capricorn. Pisceans are supposed to be imaginative, compassionate, unworldly, secretive, and escapist.

What Day of the Week is March 7?

On what day of the week does March 7 fall?

Unfortunately, this isn't an easy question. Because the calendar year is 365 days long (366 in leap years), it doesn't divide evenly by the seven days of the week.

Also, the Earth goes around the Sun in about 365-1/4 days, so a calendar tends to drift over time. That's why the same date falls on different weekdays in different years.

This is made even more complicated by a change in calendars that took place in 1582. Our modern calendar has its roots in ancient Rome, in a calendar reform conducted by Julius Caesar. Caesar commissioned mathematicians to attack the problem, and came up with the idea of *leap years*, and thus standardized the calendar for centuries to come. This was called the *Julian calendar*.

Over time, however, the small errors in Caesar's calculation compounded. That's why Pope Gregory XIII commissioned the *Gregorian calendar*, used in most of the world today. Some countries converted in 1582, when the calendar was first developed; some converted later; other still haven't changed.

Gregorian and Julian aren't the only types of calendars. The Hebrew year, the Islamic year, and many other calendars are used in different parts of the world and among different people.

You can convert Gregorian dates to other calendars, including the Hebrew calendar, the Islamic calendar, and even the Mayan calendar by visiting the Fourmilab Calendar Converter at http://www.fourmilab.ch/documents/calendar/.

A 50-year brass perpetual calendar.

Copyright, Credit, and Contact

Follow Us

Our blog Dobson's Improbable History features short articles on events and people associated with each day, and updates several times each week. Get the latest on Twitter @SidewiseThinker.

Sources and Art Credits

All art and photographs are either in the public domain or used under a Creative Commons license. Attribution is provided where requested by the copyright owner or when of historical significance, listed below.

- The cover image of "Gray Tree" by Piet Mondrian is in the public domain in the United States because it was published prior to January 1, 1923.

- The back cover photograph, "U. S. First Army at Remagen Bridge Four Hours Before it Collapsed into the Rhine" is by U. S. Army combat photographer Irwin Waxman, and is in the public domain.

- The photograph "U. S. First Army at Remagen Bridge" in the "Event of the Day" section is by a U.S. Army combat photographer and is in the public domain.

- The 1799 painting "Napoleon Bonaparte Visiting the Plague-Stricken at Jaffa" by Antoine-Jean Gros is in the public domain because its copyright has expired.

- The 1965 photograph from the "Bloody Sunday" attacks was taken by an FBI photographer and is in the public domain.

- The illustration of the Kepler Telescope is by NASA and is in the public domain.

- The 1941 painting "Girl Writing" by Milton Avery is used under "fair use" provisions because this low-resolution image serves only to illustrate a biographical description of the artist.

- The 1930 painting "Composition II in Red, Blue, and Yellow" by Piet Mondrian is used under "fair use" provisions because this low-resolution image serves only to illustrate a biographical description of the artist.

- The outline of the figures raising the flag on Iwo Jima is by "Aeoris" and is licensed under the Creative Commons Attribution-Share Alike 3.0 Unported.

- The Canadian recruiting poster "Ce qu'il faut por vaincre" is in the public domain because it was created in Canada prior to January 1, 1949.

- The photograph of Comet Hale-Bopp was taken by E. Kolmhofer and H. Rabb of the Johannes-Kepler-Observatory in Linz, Austria, and is licensed under the Creative Commons Attribution-Share Alike 3.0 Unported License.

- The photograph of Luther Burbank is from the September 1908 issue of *Overland Monthly*, and is in the public domain because its copyright has expired.

- The photograph "Le cour du domaine du Gras" by Nicéphore Niépce is in the public domain because its copyright has expired.

- The photograph of Janet Guthrie's Wildcat 3DGS was taken by Dan Wildhirt and is licensed under Creative Commons Attribution-Share Alike 3.0 Unported license.

- The logo for *2001: A Space Odyssey* does not meet the threshold for copyright protection, and is therefore in the public domain.

- The record label for "Seven Come Eleven" by Pee Wee King and His Band is ineligible for copyright because it contains no original authorship.

- The 1943 photograph of Duke Ellington by Gordon Parks is in the public domain because it was taken in his role as an employee or contractor of the Federal government as part of his official duties.

- The bust of Antoninus Pius is located in the British Museum. The photograph was taken by Jastrow, and is licensed under the Creative Commons Attribution 2.5 Generic license.

- The detail from the painting "Triumph of St. Thomas Aquinas Over the Heretics" is by Filippino Lippi and was painted between 1489 and 1491, and is thus in the public domain. The original painting can be seen at the Santa Maria sopra Minerva in Rome.

- The photograph of James "Cool Papa" Bell is from an original located at the Negro League Baseball Museum. Its copyright status is unknown, but the Negro Leagues eMuseum Library Material Usage Policy provides that "Materials on these pages may be distributed and duplicated if unchanged in format and content," and is used here on that basis.

61